THE ART OF ASSET PROTECTION

by

Brendan James Gilbert, JD, MBA

Copyright © December 2011 by Brendan James Gilbert. All rights reserved. Except as permitted under the United States Copyright Act of 1976 as amended, no part of this publication may be reproduced or distributed in any form by any means, or stored in a database or retrieval system, without prior written permission of the publisher.

This publication is designed to provide accurate and authoritative information in regard to the subject matter covered. It is sold with the understanding that the publisher is not engaged in rendering legal, accounting or other professional service. If legal advice or other expert assistance is required, the services of a competent professional person should be sought.
—from a *Declaration of Principles* jointly adopted by a committee of the American Bar Association and a committee of publishers and associations.

Certain images used with permission from the Gilbert Law Office; others are public domain except as indicated.

This book is dedicated to my father, and his advice that the need for asset protection need be made known to the average Joe (or Denny).

For asset protection planning services from New York attorneys, please visit our website at **assetprotecting.com**.

Table of Contents

Preface   ix

Chapter 1.   **LAYING PLANS—**
What Asset Protection Can and Can't Do   1

Chapter 2.   **WAGING WAR—**
How Asset Protection Planning Works in Court   15

Chapter 3.   **ATTACK BY STRATAGEM—**
A Creditor's Attack Routes   23

Chapter 4.   **TACTICAL DISPOSITIONS—**
Defending the Attack Routes   31

Chapter 5.   **ENERGY—**
Convincing the Creditor to Settle Within Insurance Coverage   43

Chapter 6.   **WEAK POINTS AND STRONG—**
How Asset Protection Plans Can Fail or Triumph   47

Chapter 7.   **MANEUVERING—**
Pre- and Post-Litigation   51

Table of Contents

Chapter 8.   **VARIATION IN TACTICS—**
Regarding New Asset Protection
Methodologies   55

Chapter 9.   **THE ARMY ON THE MARCH—**
The Time for Asset Protection
Planning   61

Chapter 10.   **TERRAIN—**
Asset Protection for Real Estate   63

Chapter 11.   **THE NINE SITUATIONS—**
Asset Protection Planning for the
Various Types of Wealth   73

Chapter 12.   **(STOPPING) THE ATTACK BY FIRE—**
Fireproof Offshore Jurisdictions   87

Chapter 13.   **THE USE OF SPIES—**
Regarding Secrecy and Hiding as
an Asset Protection Methodology   91

About the Author   95

Above and on the cover: Sun Tzu.

Below: An excerpt of the Art of War.

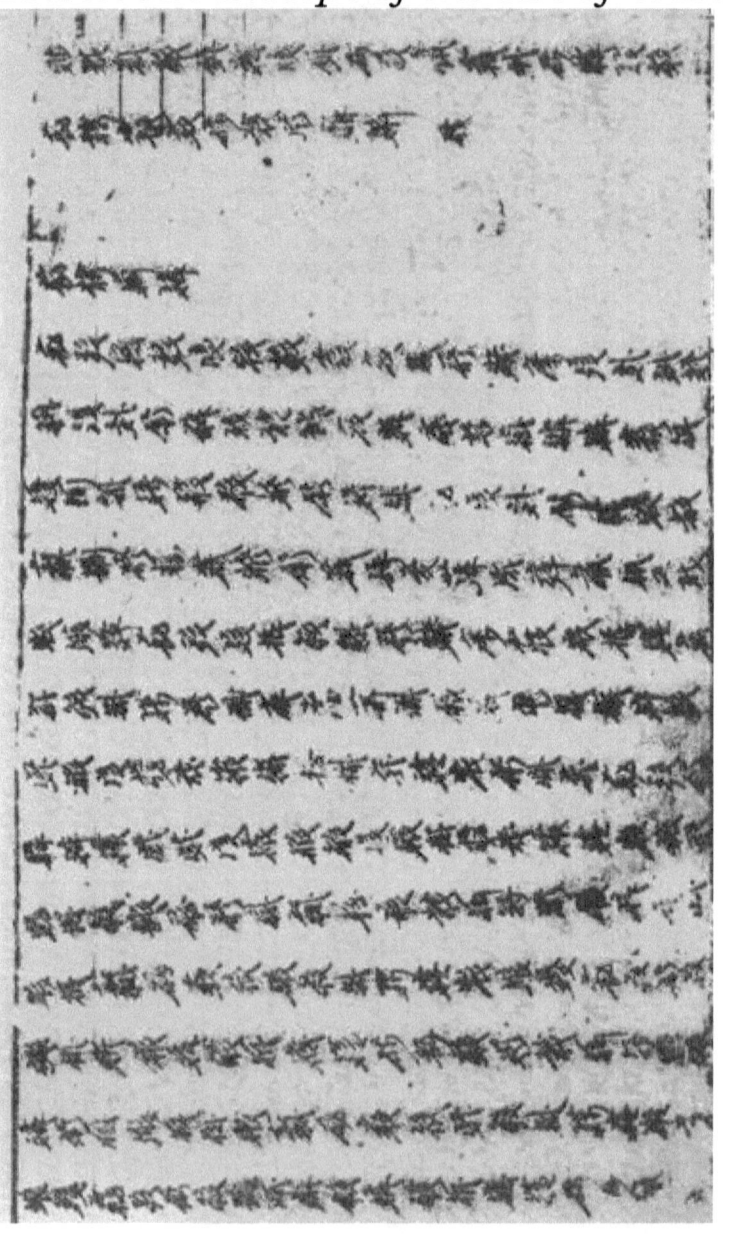

Preface

To many, asset protection seems like an ultra-luxury.

The aim of this book is to let people know **who** can provide competent asset protection planning, **what** asset protection is, **where** asset protection can be done, **when** asset protection should be done, **why** it is no longer a luxury, but a necessity, and **how** asset protection can be achieved. To this end, it is written in a (hopefully) approachable format for both the interested public and financial professionals, and should cover the broad strokes of asset protection planning in one sitting.

Simply being in America puts you at greater risk of being sued than anything else. **America has approximately 1,200,000 lawyers; 70% of the entire world's.** China, with 5 times America's population, had 110,000 in 2002.
American law students? Approximately 130,000, with nearly 40,000 graduating yearly. They're crushed by an average of **six figures of debt to pay back**, and are willing to take risky cases to do so.

Preface

Your chance of being sued this year? 1 in 5; but 1 in 3 if you are a professional or business owner.

Asset protection providers don't advertise on television. Financial advisors and retirement fund providers are the closest. They advertise that they protect your family's wealth and provide retirement security, and may do just that so long as you aren't targeted by plaintiff's lawyers.

By contrast, those plaintiff's lawyers advertise like it is going out of style. For many (blissful) years, many states and bar associations forbade attorneys from advertising due to a lowering of the perception of the profession. The floodgates opened in the past few decades, and a race-to-the-bottom ensued. They'll sue anything with legs. But a notable omission from plaintiff's lawyers advertising is collection of the eye-popping verdict, and that is because collection can be an entirely different animal.

The cost–benefit for a lawsuit weighs far in favor of the plaintiff. With plaintiff's contingent lawyers, a plaintiff is only out a

Preface

few hours of their time and court filing fees (if the lawyer doesn't provide them). If the plaintiff is successful, however, he or she gets winnings based on how sympathetic they are. If the plaintiff doubts success, they simply seek to settle and extort as much as possible. Hardly any defense attorneys can take work on a contingency basis, because the desired result is dismissal of the plaintiff's case, not a recovery from the plaintiff.

Much attention is focused on so-called frivolous lawsuits. Under ethical rules and most if not all states' rules, lawyers are prohibited from bringing frivolous lawsuits, but the definition is different from the popular definition. Having more lawyers means a higher probability that a frivolous lawsuit (in the popular definition) will be brought, as does bad economic times. You don't have to do anything wrong to be sued and forced to pay to defend yourself.

An asset protection plan shifts the costs to collect back onto the plaintiff. The plan won't win a lawsuit that's in progress for you—but it will discourage plaintiff's lawyers and plaintiffs from bringing suit in the first place, which is a better victory still to seek as a result of a plan.

Sun Tzu's *The Art of War* is used as an older-than-dirt metaphor for asset protection planning because asset protection planning in the United States **is** older-than-dirt. It is the primary way in which accumulated wealth is retained and passed down, even in the face of claims of plaintiff's attorneys. It is the secret behind the "old money" families in this country, and it is more affordable now for the public than ever. Any family with any net worth can't afford not to consider developing an asset protection plan. If you believe that you don't own enough to protect, ask yourself: How long did it take for me to pay for these assets? How would I feel if a creditor took them, and (depending on the asset) my only alternative to save it is to declare bankruptcy and ruin my credit?

Chapter 1

LAYING PLANS
What Asset Protection Can and Can't Do

Now the general who wins a battle makes many calculations in his temple ere the battle is fought. The general who loses a battle makes but few calculations beforehand. Thus do many calculations lead to victory, and few calculations to defeat: how much more no calculation at all! It is by attention to this point that I can foresee who is likely to win or lose.

Chapter 1

Above: The Longzhong Plan being discussed by Liu Bei and Zhuge Liang mural, at the Beijing Summer Palace.

In the late Han Dynasty of ancient China, warlord Liu Bei was down on his luck. Despite him being the uncle of the emperor, the emperor's power had been seized by a prime minister who used the emperor as a puppet and regarded the imperial uncle as a rebel to his authority. As this prime minister seized and

Laying Plans

consolidated his power across northern China, Liu was forced to flee from city to city, alternatively fielding a puny force or seeking refuge with other warlords sympathetic to the emperor and dynasty.

Liu met a military advisor named Zhuge Liang that laid out what came to be known as the Longzhong Plan—a comprehensive plan by which the prime minister could be kept at bay and Liu could establish a state in the southwest of China's mountainous terrain. Legend has it that through this plan and the advice of Zhuge that Liu was able to secure his place in ancient Chinese history and culture, preserve the Han as the Prince of Hanzhong, and he and his successor could carry on the resistance for decades.

Overview of an Asset Protection Plan

Like the Longzhong Plan, good asset protection planning is comprehensive and is made to accommodate the realities of the present situation (that is, how you have accumulated the wealth you are protecting and how your affairs are currently structured) and the likely course of the future (that is, future business deals, acquisitions, and investments; a retirement strategy or business succession planning; and any other changes on the horizon). The intention of the plan should be to control everything but own nothing.

It must also be understandable and explainable by you. An intricate asset protection plan does nothing but collect dust or, worse yet, get misused if you are never trained in how to use it or are unaware of how the components of the plan are meant to work together. Therefore, a significant role of the asset protection planner is to educate in the proper use of the created plan to ensure effectiveness.

WHAT AN ASSET PROTECTION PLAN CAN DO

An effective asset protection plan will induce any plaintiffs and their plaintiff's lawyers that sue you to settle within a coverage limit or to settle for an amount far

LAYING PLANS

less than a regular defendant would pay. The plan accomplishes this by making it so difficult for a plaintiff to collect a court's judgment, that voluntary settlement now for a much smaller amount is the better option to the plaintiff.

Effective asset protection planning won't win the lawsuit. The lawsuit is just the beginning. Asset protection planning wins the collections battle, forcing a plaintiff to wait years and pay tens of thousands in fees to collect their judgment, or to settle now for cents on the dollar.

Asset protection will also accomplish and work in harmony with estate planning, although unlike estate planning asset protection planning prioritizes the here-and-now. Planning will reduce gift and estate taxes in almost every circumstance, possibly avoiding them all together. In some circumstances, it can also legally apportion income tax between family members who are in a lower tax bracket, resulting in tax savings in the aggregate.

Asset protection planning is effective to varying degrees against claims made against you in divorce, from business deals and joint ventures gone bad, and from claims based on your ownership of property.

ASSET PROTECTION PLANNING FOR BUSINESSES

Asset protection can also protect a high-risk business that you own through arrangements between companies. Consider the following possibilities if you own a high-risk company (HRC):

You can have another company (possibly one you also control) own the HRC's furniture, equipment, etc. and lease them to the HRC, with a lease that can be terminated to "yank out" the assets provided in the event of certain occurrences such as bankruptcy or insolvency of the HRC—to ensure that those assets aren't exposed to the liabilities of the HRC leasing the assets, and your equity in those assets remains safe.

You can create another company to bill the HRC's customers and handle accounts

Laying Plans

receivable/collections actions that contracts with the HRC, so that the value of those accounts receivable are not considered an asset of the HRC doing the work, and so a management fee can be earned by your billing/collections company and control over when and if payments are made to the HRC.

Consider the alternative of accounts receivable factoring, allowing the HRC to borrow against its accounts receivable and thereby strip them of their value.

You could additionally create a defined benefit plan to take advantage of state and federal law protections like ERISA and ensure a protected retirement.

Finally, consider having the HRC own an insurance company or risk retention group to become self-insured, allowing the HRC's owners to collect the profits that would otherwise be paid to a third-party insurer.

It is best to carry insurance that is complementary to your asset protection plan. Your liability coverage could be reduced to an amount needed to pay for defense representation.

Asset protection is a deterrent to going beyond your insurance coverage—this way a plaintiff is likely to settle within your insurance coverage bounds, because trying to get personal assets tied up in an asset protection plan is like pulling teeth.

ASSET PROTECTION PLANNING FOR PROFESSIONALS

Asset protection isn't just for your clients. It is an integral part of protecting the practice that you have worked so hard to build and cultivate. And it works hand-in-hand with malpractice insurance.

Better yet—an asset protection plan has no annual premiums or deductibles. It is always there, and it always will be there. No worry about extended reporting periods or claims falling outside of your occurrence-basis malpractice policy.

Laying Plans

Asset Protection Planner Differences

Depending on the asset protection planners you retain, you may be afforded extra protections or benefits.

Attorneys provide the benefit of attorney–client privilege to virtually all asset protection planning discussions, independently verifiable credentials by the state(s) that license them and a partially nationally standardized evaluation of competency (even if it is of dubious value) in the form of the bar exam, possible experience with the tax code, protections and ethical requirements of the jurisdiction's code of professional conduct, the ability to represent you in court, including tax court (130,000 are admitted), the ability and available resources to perform independent legal research, the requirement of providing legal services of a reasonably-expected quality and your security of being able to sue them for malpractice if they don't meet this standard.

Accountants and CPAs provide the benefits of verification of credentials by the state(s) that license them, virtually certain experience with the tax code, potentially the ability to represent you in tax court (if the CPA has passed the exam for admission, which has an approximate 10% pass rate and is offered every other year; only 202 non-attorneys have been admitted) and the security of being able to sue them for malpractice if necessary. However, they very likely require an attorney to supervise trust creation and advise you on the trust's workings, or they risk the unauthorized practice of law. Generally, accountants and CPAs also runs the risk of believing that because they understand the tax effects of an asset protection method, they understand the legal effects as well—occasionally with disastrous results.

Financial Planners provide the benefits of verification of credentials with an institution (often the American College, which is reputable and maintains a wide swath of certifications for planners). They may use cookie-cutter trust documents

Laying Plans

that are relatively "fill-in-the-blank" style that they have had created and thus can provide their attorney's written materials about, but would require an attorney to supervise custom-tailored trust creation and advise you on the trust's workings, or risks the unauthorized practice of law. Financial planners likely are inclined to use a standardized document, are not necessarily qualified to gauge its fitness for your circumstances, and may be unable to satisfactorily advise you on whether it is appropriate for you. They are well-advised to partner up with an attorney or law office providing services in this area and refer their clients to them for all of the benefits mentioned above.

Business school graduates, whether MBA or bachelor's, could be virtually of any quality, perhaps even have a diploma from a sham online university. Knowledge of accounting and law could be as little as one required course in their curriculum or none. Proceed with caution.

LegalZoom and other websites claim that their documents have been generated, used

Chapter 1

or appropriated from attorneys. But they likely provide no meaningful analysis of your situation to the documents they offer (if they do, it is probably from "strangers on the Internet"), no privilege, and the possibility of disastrous consequences caused by the lack of legal (or any meaningful, really) analysis of the papers they generate. Proceed with extreme caution.

Average Joes burned by the system, fighting the IRS, or emulating Wesley Snipes. Please don't proceed at all.

WHAT AN ASSET PROTECTION PLAN CAN'T DO

With the large amount of providers of asset protection, there are a few planner-scammers.

Know that an asset protection plan cannot reduce your income tax liability. Anyone who claims that asset protection planning does is offering you criminal liability. Income tax is assessed based on

Laying Plans

citizenship and no trust or offshore structure changes that.

Asset protection also cannot allow you to keep and own (or exercise a significant-enough degree of control over) money offshore and be free from the obligation of having to return it to satisfy a judgment against you personally. Unless your plan is to leave the country and never return, civil courts can jail you for contempt of court and have done so for people unwilling to "repatriate" money back into the country to satisfy a judgment.

Finally, asset protection cannot absolutely guarantee protection, and any planner who makes such a guarantee should be regarded with extreme suspicion. Judge-made law and legislation, often made at the behest of creditor's lobbyists, can un-do an entire asset protection methodology or undermine a method overnight. For an example of how this can occur, please see the discussion of the Olmstead case in the next chapter.

Chapter 2

WAGING WAR
How Asset Protection Planning Works in Court

When you engage in actual fighting, if victory is long in coming, then men's weapons will grow dull and their ardor will be damped. If you lay siege to a town, you will exhaust your strength.

There is no instance of a country having benefited from prolonged warfare. It is only one who is thoroughly acquainted with the evils of war that can thoroughly understand the profitable way of carrying it on.

Chapter 2

Following World War I, imperial Germany ceased to exist. Five years of war brought revolution and the Weimar Republic in 1919. But the devastation of war placed the Republic in a state of economic depression and hyperinflation, political extremism, and capitulation and oppression from the victors of the First World War through the Treaty of Versailles.

These factors, in concert with others, led to the establishment of the Third Reich, which was able to tap into German anger from massive unemployment, desire to retake territories conceded under the Treaty and avenge their national reputation lost from prolonged warfare.

A good asset protection plan leaves the court no choice but to allow the protected debtor to escape punishment, and does not infuriate the court to such a degree that, like Germany post-Treaty, vengeance must be sought.

JUDICIAL VENGEANCE

Always, always keep in mind that an asset protection plan has to be made to

Waging War

withstand testing in court. The way it will be tested is this: a judge or jury will grant a plaintiff a judgment against you, and then you will need to convince that judge or another that the financial arrangements you have made make payment of the judgment impossible. Fanciful innovations that tell creditors and the courts to go pound salt will serve to get you pounded instead by challenged judges and result in more creditor-centric legislation.

If it is the same judge as the trial, understand that they want to render judgments that are enforceable and collectible. They will know everything that you have in accounts worth $10,000 or more from your answers in the debtor's examination. They will regard any planning that you have done with extreme scrutiny and try to find much of any way they can make you pay. Even if you are not in front of the same judge, asset protection plans are carefully reviewed by courts to find a way to break them to avenge the judgment-creditor and vindicate his rights after the prolonged warfare they engaged in to earn their judgment.

Chapter 2

Consequently, you must make sure that your asset protection plan has a good reason behind it. Adopting a plan at the same time as estate planning is a good idea for this reason; there, the reason was for tax reduction, inheritance planning, or for other accepted reasons. Engaging in asset protection just before a business deal is another good and accepted reason to engage in some financial planning. Yet another is planning for Medicaid eligibility or retirement, two areas where irrevocable trusts are expected and welcomed.

A failing of many armchair planners is in this area. An asset protection plan that flaunts its "bulletproof" nature in the face of a judge will only irritate a well-educated person, and may make them undertake the conquering of the assets protected by the plan to avenge the authority of their court.

Just because it should work under the law doesn't mean that it will actually work in practice, standing alone against a creditor onslaught. Loopholes get tied, and bad or overconfident planners make for bad precedent and angry judges.

The Olmstead Case

Consider the example set by the Florida Supreme Court in Olmstead v. Federal Trade Commission, decided in mid-2010. Until Olmstead, judge-made law throughout the country held fairly consistently that against a limited liability company, an order to intercept distributions of money to the owners of the company (a "charging order" which is discussed in detail in next chapter) is the exclusive remedy a creditor of the individual owner can pursue. Many individuals (and asset protection planners) used single-member limited liability companies in order to hold assets, based on this premise.

The rationale for this limitation was that the owners of a limited liability company should be able to use a concept borrowed from partnership law, namely, that you **get to pick your partner** in business. If a creditor were allowed to take the ownership interest of a debtor, all of a sudden the other owners of the company would be

Chapter 2

forced into a partnership with someone they didn't choose.

However, the State of Florida (unlike certain other states) had no law saying that a charging order was the only remedy that a creditor can seek, and as such, and the Florida Supreme Court was free to use any authority it desired in deciding whether single-member limited liability companies deserved this protection.

Regrettably, the Olmsteads, through their companies, happened to be operating an "advance-fee credit card scam" according to the federal appeals court. After the federal decision, the case was submitted to the Florida Supreme Court because the question of whether the Federal Trade Commission was limited to a charging order because of Florida law was a question about Florida law that should be answered by Florida's highest court.

Given that the Olmsteads were considered scammers by the federal court, they rather started off on the wrong foot in Florida. But the legal issue of whether a single-member limited liability company was

WAGING WAR

protected by having creditors be limited to a charging order against it had collateral effects. Asset protection plans and planners across the state had advocated and devised single-member limited liability company arrangements for their clients. As you can see, this one battle would be able to decide potentially hundreds more, as creditors rely on this case as precedent in their own fights.

The Florida Supreme Court, despite the existence of judge-made law from across the country to the contrary, **decided that a single-member limited liability company does not deserve protection**. They ruled that "Florida law permits a court to order a judgment debtor to surrender all right, title, and interest in the debtor's single-member limited liability company [to their judgment creditor] to satisfy an outstanding judgment."

For this reason, we recommend that an asset protection plan be revisited at least annually to ensure changes in the law do not cripple the plan's effectiveness.

Chapter 3

ATTACK BY STRATAGEM
A Creditor's Attack Routes

The rule is, not to besiege walled cities if it can possibly be avoided.

Chapter 3

In May of 1863, Major General Ulysses Grant began his siege of Vicksburg, crossing the Mississippi River to surround the Confederate forces he routed out of Jackson, Mississippi. The Union had preferred to catch the Confederates during their westward withdrawal by flanking them, but was unable to catch them in time.

Grant began by assaulting Vicksburg, and after decisive failures was forced into besieging, with support from Union gunboats. The hot summer forced a brief truce. Eventually, it was tunneling efforts and detonated mineshafts that provoked the Confederate surrender, giving the Union control of the Mississippi. Coupled with the better-remembered victory in Gettysburg the day before, the surrender turned the tide of the Civil War.

Like Grant, creditors have a wide number of options available to them to recover moneys, the availability of which varies from state-to-state. As described in Chapter 2, creditors will be able, post-judgment, to get a very accurate snapshot

Attack by Stratagem

of your present financial situation. Hiding wealth from the public won't protect you from this battle once the war is joined and your creditor can get good intelligence about your defenses.

First Attack Route

If you simply hold the money as **cash** or a cash equivalent, the creditor can generally take the judgment and force you to pay money into court to satisfy the judgment, or force you to pay directly to them.

Second Attack Route

If you don't have the money freely available, they can have the sheriff or other law enforcement officials come to **seize property** you own and sell it off and pay the proceeds to the creditor. Some property is exempt from seizure, but very little is. Investment property almost never is.

Third Attack Route

Creditors can look over transfers that you have made during anywhere between the past three to six years (again, varying by state) and seek to have them voided (that is, undone and unwound) by **claiming the transfers were fraudulently made**, and then seize the assets transferred away. Each state differs in the fraudulent transfer law applicable to it and transactions occurring within that state. An asset protection plan ordinarily needs to consider all options open, and attempt to use choice-of-law provisions to use the fraudulent transfer law best suited for the plan. However, for those who have the assets outside of that jurisdiction, or for a creditor's lawsuit outside of that jurisdiction, it is likely that the choice-of-law provision will be disregarded and the fraudulent transfer laws of the other jurisdiction applied. Any transfers that were made to "hinder, delay, or defraud creditors" is likely to be able to be voided as a fraudulent transfer.

If the assets were transferred out of the country, creditors can potentially seek repatriation of the assets, as can courts on their own initiative. If you refuse, you will be jailed by the court until you comply,

Attack by Stratagem

and debtors have been jailed for years based on this. The contempt power of any court is strong. The court will also not accept an excuse based on impossibility, namely that the transfer was irrevocable.

Fourth Attack Route

Revocable elections that you have made will be targeted by the creditor, who will seek to revoke them and claim the assets inside, whether they be a retirement plan or a revocable trust made in estate planning.

Fifth Attack Route

If you own **business interests** or stock, creditors can often compel you to transfer those interests to them in satisfaction of the judgment.

For some types of business interests, the ability of a creditor to seize your ownership interest may be limited to a "charging order," which allows them to intercept any distributions or dividends paid to you from the business's proceeds. However, the creditor has the right to foreclose on a charging order, which means that they can still assume your ownership of the business interest.

SIXTH ATTACK ROUTE

Creditors can engage in what is referred to as a **"piercing the corporate veil" analysis** against a business interest that you own, particularly if you are the dominant owner. In so doing, they claim that the domination you have over the business is so strong that the assets of the business should be considered your own personal ones and vice versa, or that the business is your "alter ego." Factors of such domination include: the absence or inaccuracy of corporate records; the concealment or misrepresentation of members; the failure to maintain arm's length relationships with related entities; the failure to observe corporate formalities in terms of behavior and documentation; the failure to pay dividends; the intermingling of assets of the corporation and of the shareholder; the manipulation of assets or liabilities to concentrate the assets or liabilities; non-functioning

Attack by Stratagem

corporate officers and/or directors; significant undercapitalization of the business entity (capitalization requirements vary based on industry, location, and specific company circumstances); the siphoning of corporate funds by the dominant shareholder(s); and the treatment by an individual of the assets of corporation as his/her own.

Seventh Attack Route

Creditors can seek **garnishments** that go directly to the creditor, whether of your income, payments of rent to be made to you, tax return refunds, or other sources.

Effective asset protection planning seeks to prevent as many of these attack routes as possible, and defend the rest vigorously.

Note that even before filing suit, plaintiff's lawyers will engage private investigators and leverage many public sources to uncover as much financial information about you to determine if you are worth their trouble and expense in filing a lawsuit. If the plaintiff has your social security number, the plaintiff lawyer's job

Chapter 3

is much easier, and they will be able to see a great amount of information very quickly about you.

Chapter 4

TACTICAL DISPOSITIONS
Defending the Attack Routes

Thus it is that in war the victorious strategist only seeks battle after the victory has been won, whereas he who is destined to defeat first fights and afterwards looks for victory.

Chapter 4

Above: The Fall of Constantinople, painted in 1499.

Many historians know that Constantinople, the great walled city and capital of the Roman and Byzantine Empire, fell to the Ottomans after a legendary siege in 1453. What is less known is that Constantinople had been sieged many, many times before over the past eight centuries. It withstood

Tactical Dispositions

each one except for the Fourth Crusade, during which the city's residents revolted and the deposed Byzantine Emperor was restored to the throne by the Crusaders.

The first attempted siege, in 626 by the Avar Khanate and Sassanid Empire, was a spectacular failure that saved the Byzantine Empire from the brink of collapse. 674 saw the Umayyad Caliphate attack the city with superior numbers and set in for a 4-year siege; Byzantine naval control kept the city supplied and winter starvation broke the siege. A return in 717 saw the siege broken by plague.

Bulgarian and Rus sieges in 813, 860 and 941 could not secure possession of the city. Civil wars and revolts in 821 and 1047 also failed.

An asset protection plan must be your walled city. And thankfully, you'll never be deposed as Emperor over your plan. Here is how to make your plan work more like Constantinople than Vicksburg.

Chapter 4

DEFENDING THE FIRST AND SECOND ATTACK ROUTES

Effective defense of these routes requires mitigation. Methods to reduce the amount of cash on hand must be strongly considered and executed far in advance of any potential claims. Consider leasing/lease-back arrangements for furniture and equity-stripping to defuse threats from this route, as well as the high risk business asset protection concepts described in Chapter 1.

EQUITY STRIPPING

Equity Stripping is identifying assets whose value to a creditor could be reduced by having another party get a legitimate lien on the asset for substantially its entire value before the creditor does. "First in time, first in right"—the creditor will be deterred from trying to get a lien on the asset if the creditor knows someone else is ahead of him or her to get the proceeds of the sale.

TACTICAL DISPOSITIONS

There are several ways to equity strip, each of which requires careful consideration to see if it is the right way for your circumstances.

For real estate, consider the following: you can mortgage the assets, creating a mortgagor's lien on the asset; you can open a Home Equity Line of Credit; you can locate a friendly entity to extend a bona fide mortgage or second mortgage (generally, commercial lenders will not lend up to the entire value of the property, and will not be a subordinate lienholder); or you can contract a commercial bank to mortgage the property, and then have a friendly entity buy the lien and the right to receive payments off the bank.

For other property, consider creating a limited liability entity owned by the asset owners as well as a different outside owner to ensure or reduce the chance of all the owners being debtors of a common creditor. The limited liability entity needs a legitimate business purpose to function in most state's law, such as investment or an operating business. In exchange for the ownership interests, the owners sign promissory notes to the limited liability entity for the value of the assets stripped, and the limited liability entity secures the repayment with a lien.

Defending the Third Attack Route

Resisting a claim of fraudulent transfer is best done with the passage of time. In nearly all states, once the statute of limitation for a fraudulent transfer action has run, you will have a nearly insurmountable defense to any subsequent assault on this attack route.

When you do not have the luxury of running out the statute of limitation, ensuring that any transfers are made for fair consideration received and never as a gift is an important way to undermine any attack coming from this direction.

Tactical Dispositions

Defending the Fourth Attack Route

Irrevocable versions of elections exist to accomplish many of these goals in estate planning and must be used if they are to provide protection from creditors. A revocable election or trust will be revoked for the benefit of your creditors.

Defending the Fifth Attack Route

Ensuring that a creditor is limited to the charging order is the best that can be done on this attack route, and there are methods of doing so for limited liability companies, partnerships and corporations. However, there does exist authority that indicates that if the limited liability company is owned by only one person, that a creditor of that one person individually can seize the interest in the single-member company.

Therefore, it is important to try to bring in an additional member to a single-member company, such that you can make the claim that your other member is entitled to pick their partner and not be forced into a company they co-own with one of your creditors.

Consider these possibilities in defeating invasions on this route: Including a provision to make the owner's interests **unable to be assigned** without the consent of all other owners, to prevent creditors from taking the interest; including a provision **removing the power to demand dissolution** or a distribution from the LLC or partnership to cash-out an owner's interest as well as other derivative rights (that is, rights of the owners individually) such as the right to request distributions, the right to request receivership, or the right to inspect the books, included by default in most state's laws; including a provision stating that owners are **not obliged to disclose the entity or the entity's assets to anyone**, and that the LLC or partnership is also not obliged to disclose assets, to provide privacy; including a provision whereby the manager can **halt distributions to a member or partner being pursued by creditors**, and

Tactical Dispositions

can make distributions on a basis other than share of ownership, so that assets may be retained within the entity and not taken or may be given to members who are not the target of creditors; and/or including a provision allocating income and losses of the LLC or partnership to provide the most advantageous reductions to tax liability across the members of the LLC or partnership.

For a family-owned company, consider including an escape clause whereby a family member can be bought out if certain events occur (such as bankruptcy) by the family company for a small payment, again, to save substantially all of the assets of the family company from creditors.

Defending the Sixth Attack Route

So long as you go to efforts to keep your business affairs and personal affairs separated, you will be able to repel any assault along this attack route. Doing so should be a component of any asset protection plan, as being able to pierce the corporate veil could result in calamity.

DEFENDING THE SEVENTH ATTACK ROUTE

Attacks along this route can only be mitigated, but they should be mitigated through an effective asset protection plan and consultation with asset protection litigators. Depending on the laws of your state, distributions may be better categorized as wages subject to garnishment as opposed to outright interception. Having rent payments go to a company that manages the property, or to a third-party that bills the tenants for the management company, will insulate the payment from being able to be claimed by your personal creditors.

EXPLOITING NATURAL ADVANTAGES

An asset protection plan should also thoroughly consider the asset exemptions provided by your state both from collection in satisfaction of judgment and also for bankruptcy. These provide very reliable

TACTICAL DISPOSITIONS

protections, and in certain states provide spectacular amounts of protection, such as Texas and Florida's homestead exemptions protecting primary residential properties from seizure.

Chapter 5

ENERGY
Convincing the Creditor to Settle Within Insurance Coverage

In all fighting, the direct method may be used for joining battle, but indirect methods will be needed in order to secure victory.

Chapter 5

In many cases, the creditor of someone with an asset protection plan is not your typical creditor.

Against a typical creditor, often the threat of bankruptcy of the debtor will encourage settlement discussions. Particularly for an unsecured creditor, who knows that most of their debt is able to be extinguished in bankruptcy with nothing to show for their effort in seeking a judgment, a voluntary payment now is better than no payment and the need to participate in a bankruptcy action. Even a secured creditor may prefer better payment terms than would be offered in a reorganization bankruptcy's payment plan.

Prior to judgment, you can attempt to persuade a plaintiff's lawyer to settle by informing them that you have structured your assets in such a way that collection will be difficult or impossible. The plaintiff's lawyer is likely to disbelieve you, however, and chalk up your claim to mere posturing to cause settlement. If, however, the settlement offer plus your defense costs here-to-now is the full amount of coverage, this may persuade the lawyer to take the offer—he or she would be a fool not to accept.

It is probably against your interest to say "No, really, have a look at this operating agreement/trust document and you'll see" because it will provide more time and advance notice to whomever the plaintiff retains to collect the judgment, whether it is the current plaintiff's lawyer or one who focuses in collections, and it will also provide them with more time to try to void transfers made on the grounds of fraud. However, if these agreements or documents come out in discovery because they are relevant to the claim made by the plaintiff, the difficulty in collection may be revealed then.

Asset protection plan creditors often know of the assets held by the protected debtor from their research prior to bringing suit, and are entitled to a whole host of more information through debtor's examinations post-judgment. And, at this point, they will certainly be able to receive any asset protection focused operating agreements or

Chapter 5

trust documents, and you will be able to make the case that settlement for a smaller amount is justified then.

The economics of having a judgment also permits the judgment creditor to seek extra-judicial or even tortious maneuverings to recover from you. Examples of such methods available to well-heeled are described in Chapter 7.

Chapter 6

WEAK POINTS AND STRONG

How Asset Protection Plans Can Fail or Triumph

Therefore the clever combatant imposes his will on the enemy, but does not allow the enemy's will to be imposed on him.

Chapter 6

There are three primary ways in which asset protection plans fail:

In the first and most common, an asset protection plan's structures are effective but the transfers made to the plan are not effective. This can occur in several ways: the transfer could be voidable under fraudulent transfer analysis, or it could be made as a gift or with no consideration, or the transfer could, itself, be incomplete.

The second way in which a plan can fail is by being ineffective from the beginning. This can be caused by planner hubris, making an ineffective or inappropriate plan for your circumstances either from an unqualified planner or a do-it-yourself attempt, or because of a protection planner's using methods that are already proven ineffective.

The third is that the plan is ineffective due to a failure to adapt to changing circumstances. Consider what happened to single-member limited liability companies in Florida post-<u>Olmstead</u>; the decision requires revisiting every plan involving a single-member limited liability

Weak Points and Strong

company to try to bandage the wound made by <u>Olmstead</u>.

Similarly, there are three primary ways in which asset protection plans triumph:

Firstly, the plan's presence itself prevents a plaintiff from bringing suit in the first place, deciding that it is better to move on to an easier target to crack, or the plan encourages the plaintiff's lawyer to settle within the bounds of insurance coverage, if any;

Secondly, the plan limits a creditor to intercepting distributions that never come, and functionally denies them any collection of money; or

Thirdly, the creditor pursues a judgment but the plan is enough to discourage the plaintiff's lawyer from continuing on and the creditor is unable or unwilling to continue to pursue collection efforts.

Which one of these results occur depend on the nature of the creditor, the nature of the claim, the judge's temperament, the sophistication of opposing counsel and

49

Chapter 6

your own counsel, the quality and appropriateness of the asset protection planning you have in place, and your activities prior to and during creditor litigation.

Chapter 7

MANEUVERING
Pre- and Post-Litigation

We are not fit to lead an army on the march unless we are familiar with the face of the country—its mountains and forests, its pitfalls and precipices, its marshes and swamps.

Chapter 7

PRE-LITIGATION MANEUVERING

The most important pre-litigation activity is ensuring that the transfers into your asset protection plan entities will withstand attack as a fraudulent transfer. To this end, you must make sure that they were for consideration (something given in exchange of relatively equal value) and that a creditor will have a difficult time showing that they were hindered, delayed or defrauded by the transfer. The transfer, to avoid a claim of fraudulence, must not leave you in a position of insolvency, defined as your inability to make payments to your creditors in satisfaction of their claims.

Creditor, at this point, has a broad definition. In virtually all states, it includes claims of a contingent or disputed nature (for instance, lawsuits filed against you, credit accounts with disputed transactions, or others) in addition to the ascertainable and quantifiable claims (for instance, your mortgage or car payments).

Maneuvering

It is also advisable to ensure that you are paying yourself a salary from any companies you control even prior to a threat, so that once the clouds darken, you can just give yourself a raise to protect income.

Post-Litigation Maneuvering

At this point, you should have broad access to methods to limit collection and control which (if any) assets judgment collections are performed on.

Depending on your state's limitations on what can be collected on by a creditor (mentioned in Chapter 4), it is likely beneficial to increase the amount of wages you pay yourself to force a creditor to garnish the wage instead of intercepting the dividend or distribution. New York limits garnishment to 10% of wages; Texas forbids it altogether.

Your creditor may resort to questionable and extra-judicial measures to attempt to find assets to seize. Expect a creditor to check your mail to see if you are getting any bank statements from offshore bank accounts, telephone logs for calls to or from those offshore banks, searching for ways to compromise online banking accounts you may have or using a packet sniffer to view data transmitted between your computer and your bank's server, or other methods to "social engineer" ways to acquire information and then inform either the Internal Revenue Service's Criminal Investigations Division to investigate you and possibly prosecute you for tax fraud and/or the court supervising collection for civil contempt.

Although these methods are definitely gray area and potentially illegal, generally the remedies to which you would be entitled are payment from the creditor. Because you already owe the creditor a great deal of money, the creditor will simply claim that any amounts they owe you for their questionable activities are only an off-set against the judgment debt you owe them.

Therefore, expect creditor's actions post-litigation to get real ugly, real fast, especially if their collection efforts are successfully frustrated by your planning.

Chapter 8

VARIATION IN TACTICS
Regarding New Asset Protection Methodologies

So, the student of war who is unversed in the art of war of varying his plans, even though he be acquainted with the Five Advantages, will fail to make the best use of his men.

Chapter 8

New methodologies are both a good thing and a bad thing.

They are good in that creditors consistently find ways and gather judicial authorities allowing them greater power in defeating existing methodologies. New methodologies are cases of first impression for both creditors and courts, and have the potential to perplex them.

They are bad in that they do not have established precedent in their favor, and therefore the court's reaction to being perplexed may be to eviscerate them.

In my opinion, an asset protection plan should use conservative methodology wherever possible. 'Possible' in this context means that when one's affairs can map onto existing methods cleanly, going with a tested and known effective method is preferable and effort should be made to fit affairs into existing, known effective methods. Older-than-dirt methods are

Variation in Tactics

good methods, so long as they work, and may be preferable to innovations.

With these caveats known, the aggressiveness of asset protection methods appropriate for you is governed by your risk tolerance, and there exist asset protection planners and methods used by them at all points on the risk tolerance spectrum.

Known Ineffective Methods/Scams

To set a baseline, there are some known scams that are still peddled despite their ineffectiveness.

Firstly, "The Pure Trust." Pure hogwash; usually marketed with the claim that it is based on the US Constitution's use of "obligation of contracts." Despite being roundly rejected by every state and every court, promoters continue to claim (until chased out of town) it will save you income taxes and protect assets in the trust from creditors, the trust does not exist and therefore will only get you smacked with

57

tax evasion and allow the creditors to have free rein. Just ask Wesley Snipes.

Aliases: "Unincorporated Business Trust;" "Constitutional Trust;" "Final Trust;" "Common Law Trust."

Exception: "Irrevocable Pure Grantor Trust," a term coined by David J. Zumpano in a Syracuse Law Review article to distinguish a grantor trust for both income tax and estate tax purposes from an intentionally-defective grantor trust, made solely for income tax purposes but defective for estate taxes.

Secondly, planners who claim to "have had their lives ruined by the IRS," burned by other trusts, etc. and have then created the PERFECT trust, all available for the low price of $X,X95.

Truth: There are several of these out there who will happily ruin your life or get you sent to prison given the chance. They'll expect payment in full up front.

Variation in Tactics

Thirdly, planners who focus their plan around secrecy, especially offshore accounts to avoid income tax.

Truth: Income tax cannot be avoided by any trust, only apportioned. Secrecy is only an effective means of protecting wealth if you want to commit perjury or flee the United States for somewhere without extradition to evade your creditors. An asset protection planner shouldn't be your permanent vacation planner as well.

Fourthly, weekend classes to become "certified" asset protection consultants.

Truth: These "seminars" typically are more like multi-level marketing/pyramid/Ponzi schemes perpetrated to snare the gullible, and generally should be avoided unless from a reputable source, such as continuing legal education.

Chapter 9

THE ARMY ON THE MARCH
The Time for Asset Protection Planning

The rising of birds in their flight is the sign of an ambuscade. Startled beasts indicate that a sudden attack is coming.

Chapter 9

Hopefully, your parents will start protecting your assets before you are born, for instance, through tax-deferred or tax-advantaged education accounts.

Aside from that, the rule of thumb is: if you have something to lose or if there's someone out there who could sue you, the time to plan is now.

Here is a checklist of good times to begin asset protection planning to get the most out of it:

☐ Before getting credit cards or signing a lease;
☐ Before buying a car;
☐ Before buying a home, condominium or real estate;
☐ Before entering a business deal;
☐ Before marriage;
☐ Before transferring property to family members;
☐ During the gestation of your child, and with every addition to the family thereafter
☐ At retirement; and
☐ Every year at a minimum to account for changes in the law or assets.

Chapter 10

TERRAIN
Asset Protection for Real Estate

If you are situated at a great distance from the enemy, and the strength of the two armies is equal, it is not easy to provoke a battle, and fighting will be to your disadvantage.

Chapter 10

Above: the Chess Pavilion at Mount Hua, within the Qin Mountains northeast of Hanzhong. Courtesy of Wikipedia.

Terrain

After many years of moving from city-to-city, Liu managed to establish himself with the territories Zhuge identified in the Longzhong Plan.

Along the northern border, Hanzhong was naturally protected by the impassible Qin mountain range, which had only a select few passes through which attacks could be made. Compared to the territories Liu held a decade-and-a-half prior in eastern China, which was mostly flat land along the Yellow River divided by lakes and streams, Hanzhong was a natural fortress.

Because of the natural defenses, Liu was able to defend his territory against superior numbers and superior leadership for over forty years. His defense was possible because of the mountains ability to reduce the number of attack routes that could be made against him. Modern asset protection does the same thing to protect land, albeit from a different aggressor.

Real estate is most effectively protected by placing it into a trust designed to hold it if a residence, or into a company designed to hold it if it is an investment property. For companies, consider Chapter 4's coverage of how to defend the fifth attack route for provisions that should be considered for a company holding investment property.

The Qualified Personal Residence Trust (QPRT)

This is an irrevocable living trust used to hold real estate for a fixed number of years. After the term has run, it is distributed to the beneficiaries of the trust (which may and often should include other asset planning entities, such as another trust or a limited partnership.) It offers both asset protection and tax planning benefits:

Firstly, because it is a transfer of the ownership of the property, a creditor going after this asset now needs to go from the debtor to the QPRT holding the real estate, providing asset protection.

Secondly, because it is a transfer today, gift tax is assessed today (or rather, for this year). The value of the transfer above the annual limit will be subject to taxation. **This has several beneficial implications:**

Terrain

Because you are retaining the right to live in the home rent-free, the value of the home is reduced for gift tax purposes, sometimes by as much as half or more, and appreciation of the home will be tax-free to your beneficiaries. So long as the QPRT is completed before the year in which the trust creator dies (and, as above, the assets are then placed into a different asset protection entity), the QPRT assets will not be a part of the trust creator's estate and can skip the long process of probate. You will still be able to take property mortgage deductions and expenses associated with the home, and the trust can sell the property and reinvest the proceeds to purchase another property. Gifts granted through your estate to your family will hopefully be in a different year, reducing your estate's overall tax liability by taking care of one of the biggest gifts in a different year than your estate. Finally, you will get a second bite-at-the-apple, and use the annual gift limit for two separate years, both this year and the year in which your estate is probated, reducing your overall tax liability.

Chapter 10

Thirdly, there is one aspect of the QPRT that some regard as a benefit and others a drawback: because the QPRT is for a fixed term of years during which you live in the home rent-free, **after the terms end the house is transferred to the beneficiaries of the trust and must be rented back**. To circumvent this, when the QPRT is made the trust creator usually leases the home from the beneficiaries beginning when the QPRT expires, and the trust creator pays a fair rent. The idea of paying this rent is disfavored by some, but does present another opportunity to transfer assets to the beneficiaries, now as landlords.

There are **three downsides**, all related to tax:

Firstly, because the real estate is a gift within one's life, the trust beneficiaries will not receive a stepped-up basis under Internal Revenue Code Section 1014(a) that an inheritor would receive. (For an option that may allow stepped-up basis, consider having the QPRT name a SPA trust as its beneficiary.)

Terrain

Secondly, if the property is mortgaged, only the equity you have in the home is gifted to the trust in the year of transfer—remaining mortgage payments are considered additional gifts to the trust beneficiaries at the time the payment is made. Essentially, this makes for a slightly more complicated tax return.

Lastly, in the event that you die during the term of the QPRT, the entire value of the home is brought back into your estate and the home must pass through probate. (This doesn't put you in a worse position than most of American homeowners, however, who did not plan to use a QPRT.)

Chapter 10

THE DOMESTIC ASSET PROTECTION TRUST (DAPT)

Although some asset protection planners may advocate DAPTs, I do not.

DAPTs are often premised on nuances of the laws of certain states, whether it is Nevada, Delaware, Alaska, Vermont, New Hampshire or Utah. Although these recently are being adopted in more states, they remain very controversial. Due to the United States Constitution's full faith and credit clause, judgments from outside that state are required to recognize the sister-state judgment of a creditor against you.

However, a state will generally not recognize sister-state judgments if they are repugnant to the public policy of the state where recognition is sought, and it is for this reason that we do not suggest use of a DAPT in most asset protection plans. Recognition of a self-settled spendthrift trust as protective against the trust creator's own creditors is contrary to settled caselaw in all jurisdictions except those few that have adopted laws

TERRAIN

supporting DAPTs. Persuading a judge in a state other than those few to recognize the law of that state and, in so doing, prevent a creditor from suing you under your state's law, will not likely succeed. Choice-of-law provisions will not necessarily be enforceable, especially if they prevent the creditor from pursuing any remedy.

Even if you do live in a state that recognizes DAPTs presently, you may move to a jurisdiction that does not in the future. In my opinion, a solid asset protection trust should stay solid wherever in the world you go.

Chapter 11

THE NINE SITUATIONS
Asset Protection Planning for the Various Types of Wealth

Sun Tzu said: The art of war recognizes nine varieties of ground: (1) Dispersive ground; (2) facile ground; (3) contentious ground; (4) open ground; (5) ground of intersecting highways; (6) serious ground; (7) difficult ground; (8) hemmed-in ground; (9) desperate ground.

Chapter 11

Family Limited Partnerships can be used to protect family businesses and real estate. Irrevocable trusts can be used, exclusively or in concert with other protective methods, for any type of asset and provide greater control.

THE FAMILY LIMITED PARTNERSHIP (FLP)

The Family Limited Partnership is a business entity that insulates liability arising from assets. Although often used to protect an ongoing business, they can also be used to protect almost any asset. The FLP is governed by a contract between the owners of the entity called a Partnership Agreement.

The term Family Limited Partnership does not appear in the law—it is simply a designation used to indicate the general characteristics within the Partnership Agreement of a Limited Partnership meant to protect assets within a family.

The Partnership Agreement is a contract and can include a wide range of clauses.

THE NINE SITUATIONS

These can and should be tailored to your asset protection needs. This personalization is an important difference between what an asset protection attorney can offer and what financial planners can offer. In short, asset protection lawyers know what can and can't be used in a Partnership Agreement.

Generally, you should make another limited liability entity the general partner of the FLP—the general partner assumes all the liability for creditors to the FLP, and in turn provides another level of security. For more elaborate asset protection plans, we further recommend making another limited liability entity the limited partner of the LP as well, and having family members own interests in this limited liability entity.

Chapter 11

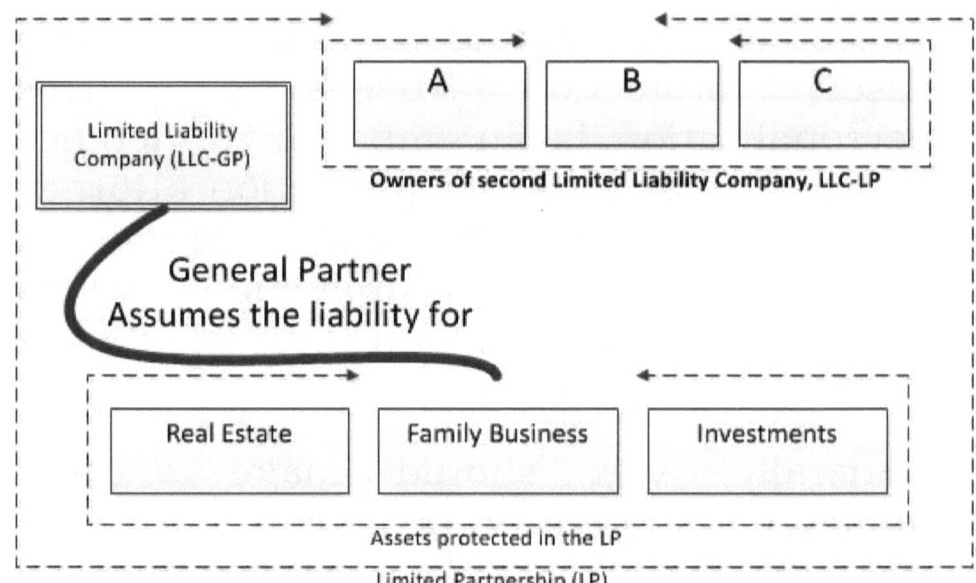

Above: the FLP.

THE NINE SITUATIONS

THE PRE-INHERITANCE TRUST

This powerful trust allows the beneficiary receiving an inheritance to exercise control over the assets prior to the grantor's death, and insulates the assets of the pre-inheritance trust from both the grantor's creditors and the beneficiary's creditors.

The grantor, when creating the pre-inheritance trust, names the beneficiary or beneficiaries as the primary, investment co-trustee and an independent trustee as the distribution trustee. Within the trust, the beneficiary is able to create companies, invest, and generally use the assets as if they were his or her own.

The investment trustee controls how, whether, and in what assets of the pre-inheritance trust are invested. The distribution trustee controls how, whether and when distributions from the trust are made. The primary co-trustee is entitled through a power of appointment to select or change distribution trustees at will.

Because this is an irrevocable trust, the assets of the pre-inheritance trust cannot be taken by creditors of the grantor. And because the assets are held in trust and the primary beneficiary does not have the power to distribute assets from the trust, the assets of the trust cannot be taken by creditors of the primary beneficiary unless distributed. The primary beneficiary can select a new primary beneficiary to receive the assets of the trust upon their death, allowing the trust to pass through to another generation without estate taxes or creditors.

And there are ways around distribution. The pre-inheritance trust could operate a business from which the primary beneficiary is employed and draws a salary, which although subject to garnishment will not be taken lock, stock, and barrel by the creditor.

THE NINE SITUATIONS

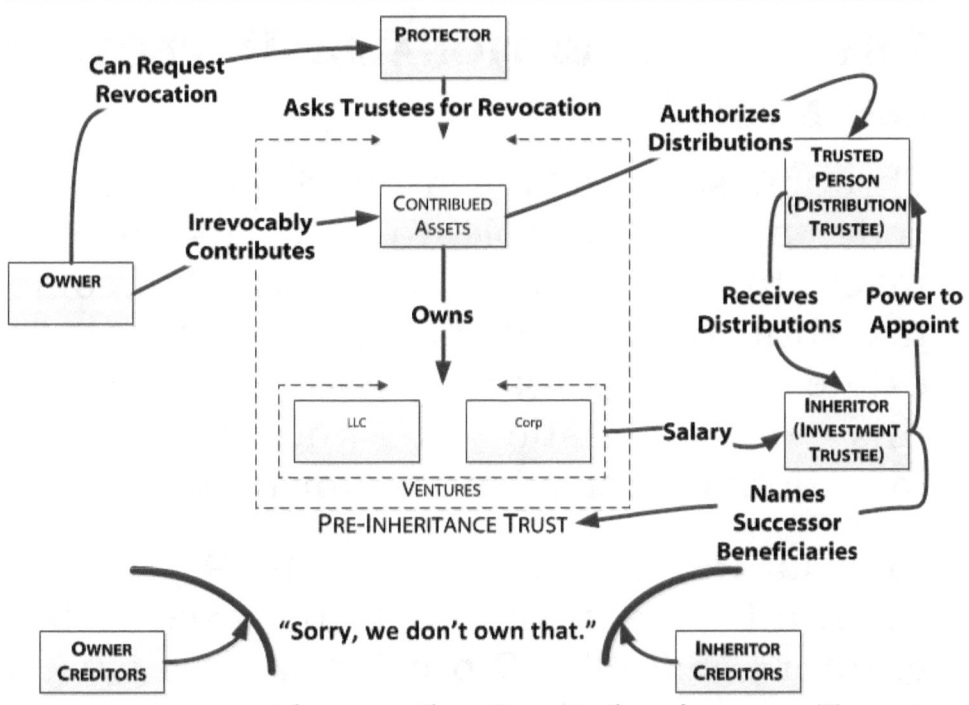

Above: the Pre-Inheritance Trust.

79

Chapter 11

THE INTENTIONALLY-DEFECTIVE GRANTOR TRUST

Through some toying around with the tax code, a trust is able to have its income taxed to the grantor as personal income tax, but be excluded from the grantor's estate for estate tax purposes. A trust with this characteristic is known as an intentionally-defective grantor trust.

Internal Revenue Code §§ 671–79 provides when a trust's income is to be taxed to the grantor. §§ 2035–42 provide when a trust's assets are to be included within the estate of the grantor at death.

Grantor trusts trigger one or multiple provisions out of each set of sections of the Code. Non Grantor trusts trigger neither set. The Intentionally-Defective Grantor Trust triggers a provision from the first set, but not the second set.

Once the IDGT is created, the premise is to fund it and have it buy assets through a promissory note that are expected to appreciate in value and are not expected to receive a step up in basis on death. Your

THE NINE SITUATIONS

house should not be transferred into the IDGT; your stock portfolio should. The transferred assets appreciate at a rate above the interest rate used on your promissory note (which uses the applicable federal rate, the lowest rate of interest possible), resulting in more wealth transferring into the trust than back into the estate. The net result is reduced gift tax liability and reduced estate taxes.

THE SPECIAL POWER OF APPOINTMENT TRUST (SPA TRUST)

This is one of the trusts used by the Vanderbilt family of railroad fame to protect their wealth, and it was a trust upheld by a New York court in protecting and managing that wealth.

The defining feature of the SPA trust is the power of appointment. A power of appointment is the power vested by the donor in a person (the donee of the power), now or in the future, to appoint someone or something (the appointee) the power to enjoy certain property. These powers can be general, meaning that the donee can appoint anyone including themself or their estate, as the person or thing to enjoy the property, or special, meaning that the donee can only appoint appointees within a certain class of persons. They can be granted over specific property or granted over all of the property within a trust.

General powers of appointment are not used in asset protection trusts, because a creditor could force the donee who exercises the power of appointment to appoint them the power to enjoy the property. But with a **special** power, because the donee can't pick themselves to benefit with a special power of appointment, they are considered not to have a property interest in the assets they have power over.

The effect of this when used in a trust focusing on asset protection is to ensure that the donee-trustee, the person who usually has this power vested in them, can only allow non-creditors to be appointees and therefore enjoy and use the property. Additionally, because this is a power to appoint someone or something to enjoy the

The Nine Situations

property and not a transfer of the property itself, it is immune from scrutiny as a fraudulent transfer by the donee-trustee's creditors. No transfer occurs, least of all a transfer to hinder, delay or defraud creditors.

For tax purposes, this trust can be considered either a grantor trust, meaning that the assets owned by the trust are taxed as though they are owned by the grantor and as if no trust existed, and pass through the grantor's estate for estate tax purposes, or a non-grantor trust, meaning that the assets owned by the trust are subject to state/federal trust taxation. Depending on the assets held by the trust, it may be appropriate to use a grantor trust. Examples abound: the taxable assessment credits given to senior home owners in life, the mortgage-interest deduction, and the step-up in taxable basis on a home owned at death.

For many clients, having two SPA trusts, one that is conventional and one that is grantor that are similar in all other aspects, is the best approach.

83

Chapter 11

Alternatively, if grantor income tax treatment is desired for the asset, but the value of the asset is to be excluded from the grantor's estate for estate tax purposes, an intentionally-defective grantor trust may be used to accomplish that.

This also has beneficial tax effects, because the value of the power to use the property is included in the appointee's estate. This means that the generation-skipping transfer tax (GSTT) is not levied against assets that pass through an estate of an appointee under a special power of appointment, so long as the appointee is within one generation or less than 37.5 years younger than the donor. Transfers made via will or probate or outright gifted to grandchildren are subject to this tax; beneficial uses granted by this Trust are not.

So long as the grantor has capacity to contract, special power of appointments can be added into existing trusts as a separate contract in order to avoid the potentially-devastating effects of the GSTT. And alternative or subsequent donees can

The Nine Situations

be named, or a class of persons can be named donees of the special power of appointment to effectively allow the trust to continue several generations from now.

Powers of appointment have been a part of the English common law for centuries. Every state recognizes them, and most have a fair amount of decided cases upholding them. It is safe to say that this form of trust is more "future-proof" than some other developing and controversial methodologies, such as self-settled domestic asset protection trusts.

Because the creator of the special power of appointment trust no longer owns the property, it does not need to be disclosed for income tax (unless a grantor trust, in which case income from the trust must be disclosed only) or bankruptcy purposes. It does not need to be revealed in a debtor's examination, revealed in the disclosure related to a divorce proceeding, or to any governmental agency. Created properly, it is not a countable resource for Medicaid eligibility purposes.

Chapter 11

For these reasons, the special power of appointment trust offers superior privacy and anonymity than any business entity used for an asset protection purpose. (Of course, having this trust own such entities, as needed, is also a good idea.)

Assets within these trusts can be used for any purpose. The trust has a taxpayer identification number (similar to a social security number) that allows the IRS to recognize it, allowing the trust to open bank accounts, investment accounts, and take advantage of virtually all financial services.

Chapter 12

(Stopping) The Attack by Fire
Fireproof Offshore Jurisdictions

But a kingdom that has once been destroyed can never come again into being; nor can the dead ever be brought back to life.

Chapter 12

There exist several offshore jurisdictions that have structured their laws such that they are debtor's havens. However, offshoring has a heavy stigma in the courts, largely because of the heavy marketing of a few with such anti-creditor laws that they make any recovery nearly impossible. For this reason, the decision of whether to offshore is a matter of risk tolerance. Even if offshoring is used, it should be used sparingly in order to avoid it contaminating a perfectly good domestic asset protection plan.

A properly configured offshore trust or business can be a strong element of an asset protection plan provided the following:

Firstly, that the assets are physically located there. For a bank, it means that there are no branch locations within the United States; other property is able to be physically located in the offshore jurisdiction to varying degrees. Certainly intellectual property would be easy to "locate" offshore.

(Stopping) The Attack by Fire

Secondly, that the offshoring is reported to the IRS. Failure to do so can result in a federal prison sentence for tax evasion. This does have the side effect that the offshore activity will easily be able to be discovered by the creditor post-judgment. The value of secrecy and hiding in asset protection will be addressed in the next chapter so that you can make an educated decision, again based on risk tolerance, of whether offshoring is appropriate for you.

Thirdly, that a reputable offshore trust fiduciary or bank is used. Offshoring isn't the lawless activity that it would appear to be, and trustworthy entities exist in every offshore jurisdiction just as untrustworthy ones do.

Fourthly, and most importantly, is that if you or your trustee retain control over property located in the offshore jurisdiction but reside in the United States, that you/your trustee are prepared to do one of the following: leave the United States permanently to frustrate collection, bring the property back to the United States to satisfy a judgment if/when the court asks

Chapter 12

you to repatriate it, or that you are prepared to be jailed until you do so. Coupled with the courts' derision for offshore accounts is their unwillingness to believe that you took your wealth, transferred it to an overseas destination, and have neither control nor the ability to bring the wealth back here to pay your creditor.

With these considerations in mind, offshoring can be very effective in that it will force a creditor to go to the foreign jurisdiction and fight the case all over again to collect, with rules stilted in your favor.

Chapter 13

THE USE OF SPIES
Regarding Secrecy and Hiding as an Asset Protection Methodology

Thus, what enables the wise sovereign and the good general to strike and conquer, and achieve things beyond the reach of ordinary men, is foreknowledge.

Chapter 13

Hiding wealth from the public is able to be accomplished through asset protection planning, but you cannot rely on secrecy and hiding to protect wealth from plaintiffs. You must assume that in the process of a lawsuit, it will come out in the open, whether during the suit (through discovery or the disclosure of relevant information to the opposing side) or after a creditor judgment or verdict.

After losing a lawsuit, you will be subject to a debtor's examination to find the extent of your assets to pay the judgment. Any accounts over $10,000 anywhere must be disclosed. Although the U.S. court will not have jurisdiction to compel the surrender of foreign accounts, the creditor will be able to go there to pursue them, and a determined creditor may do just that.

If you attempt to rely on the foreign jurisdiction's favorable laws to protect debtors, **know that the debtor's examination is under penalty of perjury**. There are legitimate offshore uses in asset protection, but using offshore accounts to

The Use of Spies

hide money from a debtor's examination is not one of them.

Many offshore jurisdictions, in addition to having debtor-friendly laws, are also prone to corruption. As mentioned in Chapter 7, a judgment creditor may resort to social engineering methods to discover foreign accounts, get information about them, and then report them to the court or the IRS for investigation to exert leverage over you if hiding the money is the primary method of protection you use.

For these reasons, concealment itself is not an effective asset protection strategy, but secrecy and hiding can be an often desirable side effect of asset protection planning.

About the Author

Brendan was born and raised in Western New York. He attended the State University of New York, University at Buffalo and received his bachelor's degree in Computer Science.

Upon returning for graduate school, he completed a dual-degree program, receiving from the University his Masters of Business Administration and his law degree.

On the side, he spent four years teaching technical matter (the development and use of databases) to over fifteen hundred management students, and administrated the University's legal assistance office during his final year.

Currently, he practices as an attorney in Williamsville, a suburb of Buffalo, and has focused his practice on asset protection planning for clients on both coasts with net worth between six and eight figures, and the incorporation of business.

About the Author

He is licensed as an attorney and counselor-at-law in New York State, and is admitted to practice to the United States District Court for the Western District of New York, the Bankruptcy Court for the Western District of New York, and the United States Tax Court. He is a proud member of the New York State Bar Association, the Bar Association of Erie County, and the New York State Defenders Association. He is also a New York State Public Notary.

He is available at (716) 222-0062 or by email at brendan@assetprotecting.com, and he loves feedback.

www.ingramcontent.com/pod-product-compliance
Lightning Source LLC
Chambersburg PA
CBHW030854180526
45163CB00004B/1569